Birdy, Birdy, What did you see?

Hollyann N. Allen

ISBN: 979-8-5964-7334-6

DEDICATION

This book is dedicated to my darling Nae Nae girl who is my reason for everything. Without that beautiful spring morning sitting outside quietly just you and me in the early hours and taking in all the life that was around us, I would've never found my other passion. One that is second only to being your mommy, to which nothing could ever compare. I love you endlessly.

Cardinal, Cardinal, What did you see?

The Cardinal is one of the most well known. The male stands out in the tree with an almost entirely red body and bright orange beak. The female, while covered in a mostly dull brown color, still displays the same red in a crest on her head and throughout her wings. She also has the same bright orange beak as a male. Cardinals can be found year round at feeders or foraging around on the ground for seeds, specifically sunflower seeds!

I saw a Blue Jay sharing his peanuts with me!

Blue Jay, Blue Jay, What did you see?

This peanut loving larger songbird is unmistakable. He and the female both stand tall in bright blue almost shimmery colors with bold black and white accents. He doesn't let anyone miss his arrival with a large defining crest on his head and noisy calls all along his way. This makes sense since a group of Blue Jays is referred to as a party! Did you know that Blue Jays' are one of the few songbird species that can mimic a hawk (which is a common bird of prey) in order to protect their young?

I saw mother duck with
her ducklings headed to
the pond without me!

Ducklings, Ducklings, What did you see?

Ducks are mostly aquatic birds meaning that they spend most of their time in the water! They are very common and can be seen on every continent around the world except for Antarctica. A male duck is called a drake, a female duck a hen and a baby duck is referred to as a duckling. Many species of ducks are migratory birds! This means that they move to warmer weather every winter, sometimes traveling very long distances to find it.

I saw a hummingbird
drinking from the nectar
feeder above me!

Hummingbird, Hummingbird, What did you see?

Hummingbirds are the smallest bird in existence. They get their name from the humming noise that their wings make while beating rapidly. Hummingbirds are the only bird that can fly backwards! You will often find them fleeting quickly between nectar feeders enjoying a sweet mixture of sugar water.

I saw a Chickadee hiding away its food in the tree limb behind me!

Chickadee, Chickadee, What did you see?

Did you know that the chickadee can find food that it has hidden away for up to a month after stashing it? This practice is called caching! It is done in preparation for the winter when food may be harder to come across. Their hippocampus, a part of their brains that helps with memory, even grows slightly larger leading up to this time to help them prepare. Chickadees are frequent feeder visitors and can often be heard before they are seen with their fun and easily identifiable "chicka-dee-dee" call.

I saw a woodpecker pecking into the tree high up above me!

Woodpecker, Woodpecker, What did you see?

There are over 20 species of woodpecker in North America. Some of the more common species include the Downy woodpecker, Red bellied woodpecker, Northern flicker, Sapsuckers and the Pileated woodpecker. Where they are found, the Downy woodpecker is the most likely to visit your backyard feeders. They prefer peanuts, sunflower seeds and even chunks of peanut butter! The male and female can be easily told apart by a bright red spot that is located only on the back of a male Downy's head.

I saw a Wren singing loudly to his mate beside me!

Wren, Wren, What did you see?

There are many different species of wrens around the world. Some of the more common types we find around North America are the Carolina Wren, the House Wren, Winter Wren and the Marsh Wren. The Wren is most commonly known for its loud and joyful songs sang at a volume that feels much bigger than the wrens small body appears capable of. The Carolina Wren will produce up to three sets of eggs, called broods, per year. They will create these nests in any cavity they deem suitable including old boots you may have left laying around outdoors, building crevices and even the wreath on your front door!

I saw a Cowbird mother laying her eggs in the nest beside me!

Cowbird, Cowbird, What did you see?

The Brown headed Cowbird is the only common species in North America that are known to be parasites of smaller songbird species' nests. A female cowbird will lay her eggs in the nest of another bird to leave the alternate species in charge of raising her young. Cowbirds can often be found in fields where livestock, such as cows, graze. This is actually where the cowbird got its name. They eat seeds from the grass and insects that on farm type land can be kicked up by the other animals.

I saw a Bluebird splashing
in the birdbath beside me!

Bluebird, Bluebird, What did you see?

There are three species of Bluebird in North America: Eastern, Western and Mountain. The Eastern Bluebird can fly up to 17 MPH. Although they are not strong enough to create holes in trees themselves to nest, most Bluebirds will often take up abandoned nests of other species such as the Woodpecker. However, like many other birds, they do depend on having a reliable water source close by in order to lay their eggs. Bluebird eggs are often replicated for decoration purposes because of their beautiful pastel blue color! Although you are likely to see these birds flying around your yard, they can be harder to attract to your feeder. They are typically insect eaters and can sometimes be lured in with food such as dried fruit or mealworms.

I saw a Robin migrating
for the winter beside me!

Robin, Robin, What did you see?

Robins are mainly resident or "short migrant" birds. This means that the American Robin can be found anytime of year throughout the entire United States. This is however only true for those the south of Canada. Robins that choose to nest further up north will move towards the US come fall, some traveling even thousands of miles! While the American Robin is a common victim to the Brown-headed Cowbird, the Robin has a special talent in detecting foreign eggs. This means that the Robin is able to identify which eggs are not their own and evict the eggs of the parasitic species without any harm to their own young.

I saw a Tufted Titmouse sounding its alarm behind me.

Titmouse, Titmouse, What did you see?

The Tufted Titmouse is small but mighty! This little grey bird has an alarm call that can be incredibly deceptive, as it appears to be fading away in to the distance. This crafty call causes the listener to believe the bird is on the move to somewhere different from their true location. The black crested titmouse, a species found in Texas and Northern Mexico, was once considered a part of the Tufted Titmouse species but was separated into its own in 2002!

I saw future birders' looking through their binoculars at me!

Birders, Birders, What did you all see?

We saw a Cardinal, Blue Jay, Duckling, Hummingbird, Chickadee, Woodpecker, Wren, Cowbird, Bluebird, Robin, and Tufted Titmouse. That's what we see!

ABOUT THE AUTHOR

Hollyann is a bird enthusiast who is blessed enough to have a husband and young daughter that support her birding passion. She has been writing on and off her entire life but actually pursued her career in marketing after attending Georgia State University. She spends most of her days on the floor building block towers and racing toy cars with her toddler.

www.ingramcontent.com/pod-product-compliance
Lightning Source LLC
Chambersburg PA
CBHW040058240726
48664CB00004B/1235